This Will Be

This Will Be

TERRY BOYLE

RESOURCE *Publications* · Eugene, Oregon

THIS WILL BE

Copyright © 2022 Terry Boyle. All rights reserved. Except for brief quotations in critical publications or reviews, no part of this book may be reproduced in any manner without prior written permission from the publisher. Write: Permissions, Wipf and Stock Publishers, 199 W. 8th Ave., Suite 3, Eugene, OR 97401.

Resource Publications
An Imprint of Wipf and Stock Publishers
199 W. 8th Ave., Suite 3
Eugene, OR 97401

www.wipfandstock.com

PAPERBACK ISBN: 978-1-6667-4093-6
HARDCOVER ISBN: 978-1-6667-4094-3
EBOOK ISBN: 978-1-6667-4095-0

05/04/22

To Larry, a loving, patient man.

CONTENTS

Religion is a Strange Land | 1
This Will Be | 2
Cri de Coeur | 3
Kindly Light | 4
God's Peculiar People | 5
A One Off | 6
Pillars of Doubt | 7
Dreaming It Up | 9
Here's to Being | 10
Sky Maker | 11
Living by Numbers | 13
Pater Noster | 14
Blindsided | 16
Faith is a Gamble | 17
Pilgrimage | 18
Incline to Baptism | 21
What's in a Name? | 22
Felix Culpa | 23
Searching out the Heart's Core | 24
The Designs of Silence | 26
A New Beginning | 28
Back-to-Back | 30
Lekhah-Dodi | 32
Being Alive | 33
Be Not Still | 34
Invisible Worm | 36
The Sting | 37
Strange Joy | 38
Miriam's Kaddish | 40
A Leaf from the Book | 41
I Pray Therefore I Am | 43
Ephemerality | 44
The Drunken Duck | 45
Where Angels Fear to Tread | 47
This Truth Will Not Set You on Edge | 49
Freedom | 51
A Sympathetic Fusion | 52
Passing Shadows | 53
Hide and Seek | 55
Not a Word | 56
Blank Stare | 58
Raptured in Yellow | 59
The Nightingale's Song | 60
Strange Fire | 62
Temple | 64

RELIGION IS A STRANGE LAND

Religion is a land of ancient memories,
We go there with the hope of regaining lost innocence.
Sometimes we go there for inspiration, believing in its power to restore.
For many, religion is redundant, a repetitive echo of wishful thinking.
It's for the mad ones who want to believe in a different outcome.
You cannot live there, as much as you might want to.
Within its ethereal space, its reality exists as merely a shadow.
Sometimes, we catch glimpse of its wonder while in prayer,
Just before its beauty withers and falls back into memory.

THIS WILL BE

The moment of the hour of the day
When my words will not fail me,
The month in the year of a quiet decade
When life does not pass me by once again.

> This will be

A caveat to myself to not fall in love,
An opportunity to reform my seafaring heart,
And to not dock my hopes in turbulent waters.
But to seek instead a godly wind to guide me.

> This will be

A rare occasion to glance back at this life,
And deny the usual impulse to look away
From the wake of my rippling existence,
Trailing as it does, unevenly, and unpredictably behind.

> This will not be

Another New Year's resolution,
Another well-meaning message in a bottle
Fated to be swept out to uncharted waters
To be read and tossed away by a people
Hungry for food, and for whom words
Have little meaning.

CRI DE COEUR

(Psalm 121)

I will lift up my eyes
Above the morass of hyperbole and politicking,
Lift up my gaze
Beyond the nonsensical behaviour of the self-absorbed,
Elevate my consciousness
To the mountain peaks where I still seek out El Shaddai.

For when I look to the mountains, I perceive nature unmasking,
Revealing to me the invisible face of the Creator,
And, I no longer feel the weight of loneliness.

I shall never stop looking to the hilltops for my help,
Never stop seeking out the imperceptible,
Faithfully, hoping to find solace to this question of existence,

In lifting my eyes, I am able to be free of tyranny of self,
Beholding instead the lively miracle of a celestial mystery.

And, in that place, where my soul vision is divinely focused,
I will bless the Godly traces of benevolence and love,
That mark all my comings and goings.

KINDLY LIGHT

Tonight, I find myself gazing up at a field of stars,
Bright nightly blooms lighting the dark way ahead,
I'm told, romantics cannot abide living in the real world,
Preferring to translate their soul's curiosity into words,
Longingly, aspiring to be a twinkle in God's eye.

Needlessly, my heart has for too long fasted itself of beauty,
Choosing to indulge in the persistent worries of the day,
My famished soul wasting away in daily drudgery,
But, tonight these little signs of light nourish me,
Replenishing, those minutes, hours, the real world has eaten.

GOD'S PECULIAR PEOPLE

Slumbering into consciousness, awakening to another day,
I give thanks,
Outside, bird songs celebrate the dawning of a new day,
They too rejoice in the awakening,
A heavenly breath of light emerges from the waters,
Separating us from the nightly shadows that have taunted us,
Empowered, by breath and light, my calling is renewed.

Turn the world upside down, honour the humble,
Celebrate those who lead with gentleness and kindness,
Believe in those who work selflessly,
Become a bright light to those in dark places,
For in doing so, I turn the world inside out,
In changing the plight of others, I am transformed.

On this new day, I approach the holy place without fear,
Sing and dance, with those who are full of divine fire and light,
Contend with the source of all life in unceasing prayer,
Joining my voice to the chorus of the liberated,
I, who am honoured with the gift of life by the maker of all things
Am blessed to be counted among God's peculiar people,
And I am not afraid to extend my hand to help and be helped.

A ONE OFF

As an older man, Mr. Moses has a lot of miles on him,
To me, he's ageless, divine engineering at its quirkiest,
Something powerful sparks in the engine of that heart,
Full of enough mysteries to lubricate his fine-tuned brain,
To some, Moses' passionate exuberance can be overbearing,
Like a mighty big rig trawling behind a humble motor car.
It's sad that they don't make them like him anymore.

Nowadays, we have slick, consumer-friendly models,
Designed by an algorithm to cover a wide demographic
The inner capacity meeting the normal range of standards,
Gears to satisfy, they are responsive to the slightest touch,
Consuming lackluster hearts with buffed-up glorious sheen,
Replaceable, these models are paced with developing trends,
Durability is not a prime factor in a fast-changing marketplace.

Mr. Moses does not always drive me where I want to go,
He can be demanding, taxing my limited concentration,
There are no whistles and bells to disguise poor quality,
He's reliable, dependable, enduring beyond his time,
Armed with a handbook in metaphysics, I'm forced to think,
While his almighty rig pushes my humble motor towards a
Vast endless horizon.

PILLARS OF DOUBT

Here I am God, creviced between table and wall,
Sitting with Moses in the Promised Land Diner.
Watching, as the Shekinah passes between us in a
Gentle pillar of coffee steam.
Our choice of strength, cliched and obvious,
Bold for the big man, creamy froth for me.

Pointing at the milky residue on my lip,
He strikes the table twice, laughing heartily,
Matches your glorious white hair, or what's
Left of it,
He's never been a man who minces his words,
And I fail to see why I like spending time with him.

Precariously balancing a salt cellar on a line of salt,
I catch his attention, he's prone to distraction.
It's a neat trick, leaning unsteadily like Pisa,
As he leans into my construction, he examines it,
That says it all, our lives are no more than that,
It's a miracle any of us are alive given the odds.
The whole bloody planet is balancing on its axis,
At any moment, a greater force could . . .
Shaking the table for dramatic effect, he sighs.

Sweeping up the salt into my hand,
I hesitate, left or right, which is it?
Scrutinizing my indecision, he smiles,
Reason is very fragile, always balancing itself
On the edge of superstition.

DREAMING IT UP

I have climbed up and down mountains
All my life,
It's never been about the climb nor the goal,
It's always been in search of something more,
In all these treks, my heart has never been transfigured,
And, no voice, but my own has kept me on track.

Angels ascend and descend
On the ladder of my dreams,
They know my longing so well,
I watch as their wispy forms
Float away,
Leaving no trail to follow, no sign, no trace,
Only a sneaking suspicion I'm dreaming
It all up.

HERE'S TO BEING

We are born with a mask
And, with each year a new persona emerges,
Each decade welcomes a host of new characters
The usual suspects disguising our fear of the ordinary,
Together, they search out the quirks and peculiarities of a saint
Whose quixotic charms fail to make a lasting impression,
Charging against the slings and arrows of the trivial
We quickly and quietly are pointed towards predictable banality.

Staging our lives with so many personae is costly,
Stifling, as it does, the authentic impulse to unmask,
While the infinite grace of being becomes estranged to us,
In a silhouetted world of malformed shapes.

Hiding in its infancy, its life born out of eternity,
A soul, my soul, awaits a time when age can give
Birth to wisdom, when I can be free to shed
The falsity of form and love of embellishment
To become something less and something much more.

SKY MAKER

This morning, a sky danced before me,
Soliciting me with its usual charm
Billowy clouds, fluffed and puffed up,
Donning a new, bespoke, one-off, vision,
Of another glorious day, another mystery unfolding,
Rousing the soul into awe,
To be born out into a ferocious joy,
Created by a wonderous magician,
Who pulls me out by the sleight-of-hand,
Playfully, as pulling cloudy rabbits out of a hat.

My heart, in giddy gladness, applauds,
With child-like delight and amazement,
Devouring each moment of photosynthesis
Before it evaporates and evolves
Into another moment, another reality
Changing what's before and consuming what's after.

This silent metamorphosis stirs up my spirit,
Resurrects me in an opulent sadness,
Teases me with colourful, lush, reddish notes
Written, for all to see, in glorious heavenly script,
Charming me with its inscrutable charisma,
I can feel you in the marrow of my soul.

Suddenly, beautiful wonder is heartlessly consumed as
A world of productivity begins to stir
Its engine-heart reverberating,
Hollowing out the best of my exquisite solitude
Without abashment or awareness
And no regard for the angels and their ethereal hymns,
With no regard, the monster rips, tears apart
The mystical cord that twitches inside me.

And, as if by magic the disappearing trick of the divine magician
Works perfectly,
Against the incessant whir and hum,
The angelic illusion vanishes without a trace.

I am bereft of insight, burdened by sound,
But my memory is blessed.

Let their engine soul roar,
Let them dismiss the power of those wispy angels,
With piston lungs expelling smoke and ash,
They must affirm the void in strident, passionless rants,
Their discordant voices a horror to the soul's musical flair,
While I remember the enchantment of the morning,
When I became lost in the dream of the sky maker.

LIVING BY NUMBERS

OMG! I'm back at the diner for derelict souls,
OCD Moses is counting cracks in the wall,
Mathematics, he says, is the highest form of philosophy,
There is, he informed me, a tribe of metaphysical
Accountants who are trying to calculate divinity
On a Babel abacus, and it seems they're failing,
(He's weird).

Last week, he gave a list of ten important things,
Something for you to ponder.
(He adopts this serious tone when it concerns numbers),
Ten, why not one, or two?
I hate asking him anything,
Speaking from on high, he assumes a patronizing air,
(I'm sure it kills him to come down to my level).

Did you read it?
Ten ways to be a do-gooder, yes, I did,
Did you read it knowingly?
I refused to answer that comment.
How many cracks do you see in this wall?
(Silence is the good friend I frequently ignore on these occasions),
I bet you'll tell me,
I counted 613 cracks but it's all just numbers,
You saw ten prohibitions, just as I saw cracks
And, not the wall, we're all blinded by numbers.

PATER NOSTER

To be secluded, isolated from those we love,
Is to be called to face our true humanity,
Witness who we really are,
We who have been humbled by something so small, so deadly,
Must reckon with our fragility,
Look into the abyss of our own making,
As the edge of its canopy of darkness spreads over us.

In solitude, we seek out faith,
Far beyond the dangerous idol of the flesh,
We dare not touch, breathe on another, for fear
Of the invisible germ that eats at our pride.
Death clings to us,
In each droplet of decay, it divides us one-by-one,
While politicians count us off as currency
One-by-one,
The numbers rise as we fall, still . . . .
In our souls we find true value.

Amid the clamour of knife, fork and gun,
Survival and anarchy,
The soul stirs from its despair, stretches upwards,
Towards an unseen hand,
And a godly breath pumps into its weary lungs,
Untainted, uncorrupted by vanity and greed,

Alone, in the solace in prayer,
The source of life requires no social distancing,
One-by-one, we continue to choose to be counted
Among the choosing people of faith.

BLINDSIDED

A comet travels into our space unlike any other,
And into the social stratosphere a hope-meme goes virtual,
We are not alone,
A virus invades our world unlike any other,
Pushing us further and further away from each other,
Soon, fear, racism and hatred plagued our hearts,
And now we only wish to be left alone.

Was the palace full of light or on fire
When Abraham took to his feet?
Fear makes us lonely,
Journeying inwards we constantly cross ourselves,
And, wander . . . .
Through the deserted desolate plains of existence,
Bereft of understanding, blindly scrambling for comfort,
Placing our hope in a space rock unlike any other.

Some see it as the face of God orbiting around us,
Others, an angel of light,
I see only the dark shadow of fear,
Terrorizing us as we clamber over one another
Looking to find a suitable escape route.

Defying reason, abandoning comfort,
I refuse to beat my faith against a rock,
Choosing instead to seek out the One
Who muddles and obfuscates the known,
Whose intangible divinity lives and breathes
   Among those brave enough to divest themselves of certainty.

FAITH IS A GAMBLE

So, what is faith?
I know I'm a masochist for playing this game,
Mr. Moses gets this look when he's thinking,
Like some Vegas player weighing his odds,
Is this deal worth raising the stakes for, or not?
Maybe, it was a bad decision, on my part,
To play the leap of faith card.

What do you mean by faith? Belief in God?
Volleying with a question is not surprising,
(He's the master of obfuscation)
Yes. Do you believe in a higher power?
Beards are clever disguises but the eyes
Tell a different story, and his were listening.

When I was younger I believed absolutely,
And now, it's a lot less and a lot more,
I'm not a poker player but I know a move
When I see one. Is he calling my bluff?
In my younger years, I believed Rivers
Parted before me, and the voice of God
Spoke to me, but nowadays, he mused,
I awake each morning and breathe in
The blessing of being, and I'm grateful.

PILGRIMAGE

Santa Fe you surprised me today,
Just when I thought I had you worked out
As a mere riddle in the sands,
Full of dried out dirt
Empty of meaning,
You stump me,
Throw down on my Damascus seat.

Blinded by intense heat,
I fall passively in sync to your heartfelt delirium
Hoping for a more benevolent greatness
To assuage the arid visions of dust and stone.

Lost.

I hear or feel the Shaman's incantation,
Drunk with fire and madness,
Calling to me,
Dragging me reluctantly down the spirit path
Pitiless and uncompromising.

With an angelic strength
He holds me in the womb of his imagination,
His song, deliciously wrought with guttural
Enunciations,
Filled the aching spirit that longs to be birthed.

Struggling to breathe,
To cry, hankering to see beyond ordinary sight,
Hungering to share in the star dreams of his people,
Scream! scream! scream!

New air, new thoughts, even new words
Beset this hop-scotch mind of mine,
The shudder of that electrifying moment
Passes over me again and again,
Troubling, disturbing, fighting with and against me,
Until I am forced to rest,
Compelled to stop playing the mind games,
And become present, aware of everything.

Lavender perfumes the sidewalks,
Narrow streets are alive with
Bee-loud pollinators,
I watch as the colours dance before me.

Alive.

In the dust,
I walk heart-warmed by new words
Twirling around my giddy head as I
Fumble for a fragrance phrase
To make even a broody Solomon
Smile,
But, only one word,
Stubbornly, relentlessly, seeks me out,
Tenderness.

It flits around me like a humming bird
A small, fierce, totem of this new language,
Will I be swayed?
Can I let the gentle, still, magical word tame
The brute language of my beloved chaos?

Heart-led, I let my hand
Gently glide over the swathe of purple,
And green,
Feet crossing over the cracked pavements
Thoughts dividing into cavernous faults,
Until something sacred possesses me.

A smatteringn of tiny flowers gathered in the shade,
Defiant as Spartacus,
Standing their ground under the shade of Hollyhocks
Arrayed in a cloak of many colours,
Unashamedly, welcoming my hummingbird spirit
Tenderly, nodding to me in quiet gentle repose,

And, with equal poise
A statuesque lady clothed in stars,
Ascends to greet me,
Her dark earthen, hues
Framed by starry icons
Her beauty, gloriously graceful,
She watches me foolishly flit about her,
Her sun beaten face remains unchanged,
The outstretched arms welcoming my flight.

INCLINE TO BAPTISM

I stand at the altar
Watching as the steam
Enfolds this likeness into its misty shroud.

The day begins . . . .

With the simplicity of water playing metaphysical,
Teasing my imagination, in the ordinary sense,
To bask in the familiar element substance of things.
In the clean water that lies beneath me,
I find a host of religious metaphors.

Dipping my hand into the tepid water
Ripples scatter outwards,
As the lure of my senses beckons me inwards,
Forcing me to reckon with the familar image,
Unshrouded.

Face foamed, the razor elevated in high ritual,
I resist the easy compulsion to destroy.

Fluidly, the blade slides over rough flesh
Smoothing out the prickly traces of time,
Until a nick
Drips its small sacrifice into the watery pit.

The day has begun.

WHAT'S IN A NAME?

From the dirt of creation, you made me,
Called me by name,
Loved me as the apple of your eye,
Sacred, forbidden, tempting to behold,
I was chosen to stand apart, while longing
To be one with a tribe whose names
Were unsullied by my false diffidence.

You raised me like Cain
To be the odd one out,
I tended to my own business
Befriending all but myself,
Silent among a multitude of voices,
I found no cure in Gilead
For the festering craving
To be loved as one
Among the cool cadre of equals.

Named at the breaking of waters,
Celebrating the freedom to choose
I, the fruit of your womb strayed
From the path,
Exiling myself from your native sun,
Cursed to wander the earth,
My lot was cast with the angels at Sodom
Where I was doomed at the cross for being
On the wrong side.

FELIX CULPA

My dreams have journeyed through a lifetime,
Shape-shifting into the shape of any given reality,
Awakening me to the hidden possibilities of every one,
Enticing me onto the threshold of hope to believe,
And I cannot discern if visions offered are bait or reward.

Dreaming allows me access to delightful exotic places
Pastures greener, intuited, colours, vibrantly sensual,
Pure ecstasy finds my feeble wit swooning with pleasure,
Delirious, I fear the treachery of such wonderous beauty,
Grasping the nettle, a poisonous sting surges through me,
Its pain, a natural remedy for my paradise-seeking ways.

My talent for shape-shifting has journeyed a lifetime,
Following dreams has shaped the borders of my reality,
Through the doors of perception, I have naively ambled
And blinded by longing, I rush into every secret garden,
Blooming with pride, flush with avarice, I'm ripe, ready to fall.

SEARCHING OUT THE HEART'S CORE

The origin of our meeting is quite clear to me,
It was at a library (soon to be a dinosaur of the past)
Browsing the deserted aisle of books on why God matters,
Sandwiched between the self-actualization texts,
Is where I encountered my soon-to-be mentor.

I'd recently begun to reacquaint myself to religion,
Not the stuff of rote and ritual but the essence of faith.

Mr. Moses was and still is a large presence,
Who was in my way, oblivious to my hovering.
Good manners were and still are lost on him and despite my non-too subtle hints,
I interjected myself into his search among heavenly volumes,
And, just when I thought my abruptness had failed to register,
He spoke without looking at me,

Is there any one book that would help you understand God?

The bible? Bhagavad Gita? Chinese philosophers? Koran?
All were listed alphabetically quite neatly in front of him,
Ignoring this idle speculation, I intruded further into his space,

There's no book that can do that. If you're looking for the truth,
It's inside you. These words point you back to yourself,
The start and end of your journey happens right here.

In a second, when the clarity of those hazel eyes met my own,
I saw myself as an empty thing, tired of being,

God isn't a transcendental escape from ourselves,
God is not an intellectual diversion from living,
God is an empty concept if we don't look inside,
And, face the contradictions of our nature.

I saw myself clearly that day and, for once, didn't turn away.

THE DESIGNS OF SILENCE

When I was younger, I looked to the mountains,
Up to where Dragons, trolls and God lived,
A wonder to myself, I could not be subdued,
Racing through wet grass into the vast emptiness,
Leaving the immutable silence to drown in the
Gurgle of my muck-soaked heels,
Watching the green grass rise again beneath me,
Watching as it rallied against my heavy foot pace,
But the quietness always out-paced me with its complete stillness,
The craggy, dull face of hills refused to entertain my joy,
No matter how loud I called for impermanence and change.

Dancing hormones sees the adolescent looking inside
Where monsters, demons, and God lives,
Glam, punk, new wave romantics, defy the past,
Sparkling, spitting, serenading my virile body is at play,
Vainglorious tales of conquest falling short of the mark,
Lungs full of fire and smoke see no foe vanquished
Except for the challenger, the unnerving stillness,
Silence refusing to dance to the tune I've set it,
Does not react, or respond, to my charm or ridicule,
Passively, mocking my rebellious grand gesture.

As a young man, I laughed at my childish arrogance,
The future was where my hope lay, cradled in knowledge,
Ideas, frightening, profound, sensual, enticingly free,
Leading me to philosophers, poets, artists, unrestrained, unquiet,

Who know me better than I know myself,
In my head, their monstrous ideas joust and spar with each other,
Gods and heroes alike, ponder, muse, make their heaven hell
And their hell heaven, until nothing exists, or matters,
Silence is now studious, objective, tamed by contemplation,
In-between the cracks of ideas, silence indifferently nods off,
Untouched by the lonely soul drowning in the intellectual tides.

My heroic gestures have since mellowed into ordinariness,
I still look to the mountains hoping for a sign,
My lungs are not what they once were,
There's no fire in my words, and my jousting days are done,
Silence is no longer an enemy but no friend either,

I am willing follow its quiet lead into the unknown.

A NEW BEGINNING

A garden center is a pleasant change from the usual,
I'm no gardener but if it makes Moses happy then . . .
To Eden we'll go and hang out with ageless hipsters.
I can see him eyeing up some fruit trees for his garden,
While I'm faking the appearance someone interested,
Latin and common names, I'm saying nothing,
Ignorance is a *Felix culpa* for people like me.

An apple-eating woman asks if I would like to see
Some exotic plants,
Moses wanders back to me like some homeless guy,
Miscalculating the two of us as a green-fingered pair,
She wonders if we'd like to check out the stone Buddhas,
Moses (prone to expletives when it comes to idols)
Does little to spare the feelings of the fat concrete man.

Oblivious to her assumptions, Moses points his stick at me,
See, this place is flawless, everything is damn perfect,
Go outside and there's dog shit on the sidewalk.
I'm pretending to read about the glory of a broken morning,
It's unreal, picture-perfect, now how did this inside become
That outside?
A self-satisfied stone angel has the audacity to grin at me,
We made outside like that, we're the ones to blame for that.

The apple woman, fearing the worst, fakes she's needed elsewhere,
And quickly disappears down a serpentine path,
That's it, we can choose to have this paradise here or that out there.
Another stone angel greets my smugness by sticking out his tongue,
Did she think we were gay?

BACK-TO-BACK

*To my friends at JRC who incidentally, accidentally,
gave me the space to think. Thank you.*

Complete with a panoramic view, I'm at the back
Waiting for the magic to happen.
A bystander to an ancient mystery creeping into the now,
I watch as tallit and kippah adorn their secret thoughts.
Niggun and butterfly songs emerge about me,
Unfolding from the chrysalis of each heart,
And, in the divine chaos, they randomly flutters around me,
Harmonizing with an unseen chorus of voices
The distant past encircles me in a sacred enchantment.

Week after week, I sit in the back pew,
Waiting for the mystique to grow old, worn-out,
But it is I who is growing older,
It is I whose soul continues to ascend Sinai,
To commune with tribes, known and unknown,
Speaking to me in that primal tongue-
The language that calls to the heart of me,
Calls upon me to listen,
It moves gently across the inner tabernacle,
Sings proudly to the marching élan within.

Over a year has passed,
I'm still at the back of the synagogue,
Abraham speaks to me now as if I'm some Melchizedek,
Naomi, chitters on about how Ruth and I are alike,
Moses prescribes two tablets a day
To stop me digressing.
There is no end to the backbenchers, who,
Like myself, are charmed into this quiet flight,
I wonder if Hagar minds me borrowing
Her name for the all-seeing righter of wrongs.

I'm seem to be always the back end of things,
Where everything seems to be backwards,
The end is the beginning, left is now right,
I am forever undone and mystified by these rites,
Left to bask in wonder of the source of all things,
Who watches from the back of me
While I attempt to construct wings of my own.

LEKHAH-DODI

Shabbat creeps up on my usual week
With the tenacity of a zealous bride,
And, I am caught unawares by her intrusion.
Dusk, falls casually into the warmth of lighted candles
And, flickering, a divine shadow plays
Along the chambers of my mind.
And the world around me begins to quieten
As I take a sudden intake of breath,
Open the doors of my heart to her
And I am gladdened by her insistence.

For her beauty frequently disarms my impatience,
My frenetic soul rests calmly under her canopy,
Ruth, and others who have become tribe, also dine there,
Moses, of course, tries to overstuff me with instruction,
The prophets continue to dazzle me with visions of wonder,
David's divine poetry reminds me why I love words,
In all of these things I see my beloved's finery
And, remember why it is I always welcome her in.

Through the morning blessings
My eyes are opened, anew, to the hills,
My silly scornful manner relaxes into her gift of peace,
And, I thank her for the intervention,
I thank her for imposing her presence into the tedium
Of those less meaningful chores,
And, my gratitude, spoken in litany, calls me back
To become one with the source of all life.

BEING ALIVE

And, how is Mr. Everyman's earthly condition?
Mr. Moses asks questions in the most circuitous way,
Mann is the other half's moniker, but I get the allusion,
Or, should I say, Everyperson, isn't that, politically right?
Schooled, as I am, to search for microcosms, I know,
This *particular* is ripe for burgeoning into a *universal*,
Small talk with Mr. Moses is something akin to a
Beckett play but with a point.

He's contemplating the horrendous state of the planet,
The end is nigh, and, we (the abyss-bound lemmings) are doomed.
You know how modernists are, warding off happiness
With a Nietzschean quip, devouring all of Woolf's sadness,
And, please may I have *some more* tattooed on their foreheads,
Hope has never demanded a crumb from his empty soul,
So, he's good, same old, same old.

My, my, so much energy and faith simply wasted,
It requires everything you have to believe in nothing.
You should get him into the works of Emerson,
There's someone who sees life beyond the veil of nature.
Beauty a good way to revive a person's sense of awe,
Even in the ugliest situations imaginable there are
Miracles in the smallest acts of kindness and grace.
And, stop twisting his drawers with witty sarcasm.

BE NOT STILL

Be not still heart of mine,
Resist silence and loudly beat your big drum,
Stomp, shout, scream your vibrant anthem,
And, when hoarse with the fluctuations of time
Let the chamber music of your soul echo
Through those life-giving arterial spaces.

Let me feel the swell of your rage,
Deafen me in arias, tragic and sublime,
Play no requiem, no dirge, while you throb,
Pulsate, as the mighty breath of God shakes
The very temple of your being.

Do not slow down when time races,
Keep far from the great sleep that bewitches us all,
And, don't stumble when loved ones' lull and pause.
Pray for life, not subsistence, vigor and hope,
Stifle any regret your breast inclines towards.
Lap for lap, give time its lead but do not follow
Passively in its wake.
Ignore the diminishing road behind, and go forward,
Face the finish line with the breath of God
Burning still in your lungs.

Do not let the youth make you feel a stranger
When you have never felt at home.
Make your strangeness sublime, intricate and foreign,
Speak the language of tomorrow, not yesterday.
Do not let the courtesans of today make you disappear
Into a pension, dignifying you in platitudes, bullying you
Into silent retreat.
Never relinquish, nor resign to the last gasp
Dance through the creaks and aches of your bones
Until the breath of God parts the red sea before you.

INVISIBLE WORM

'I only speak to lonely people', she said,
'Hospitals are full of them,
People without a soul to care for them'
My case was not so obvious, apparently,
Stretched out among a throng of visitors
Any comfort registered as nil by mouth.

I watched as her volunteer heart sauntered away,
Watched as the gap between us widened,
Nothing earth-splitting, this one gap among many,
Unseen, invisible to the naked eye,
Small lesions of petty impolite severances, fractured
Over time.

I speak to the lonely people,
Only visible to the naked heart, obviously
People whose lives are full of subtle divisions,
Whose hearts lie not on a sleeve,
Dwelling unseen in the clamour of the throng,
Their muted cries deafened by the sound of others,
While the invisible worm devours at the crust of their separation.

THE STING

Outside of time and space a great soul pervades all created things,
Secreting the divine essence in our dreams and our daily wanderings,

I wish I could attribute that thought to Mr. Moses,
If he had said it, the universe would've smiled,
But it was I who posited the idea of an infinite force,
It was I who wedged us in with the paradoxical question of being.
And regardless of how the universe feels about it, made me smile,
Though Mr. Moses appears to be only mildly interested.

Swatting a wasp that refuses to stop nagging him,
Moses plucks and holds up the insect's object of attention, a flower,
Beautiful isn't it? Common to those in the know.
The snobbery of doyens, the supposed experts in their field.
Knowledge is wonderful, elitism is not, knowledge hurts,
Since it solicits the many but is sadly welcomed only by the few
Who cannot stand the thought of being commonplace.

As he's speaking, the gaping mouth of silence opens,
And, devours the remaining nectar of my pretty rambling.
Was I being upbraided and demeaned by my friend?
I allowed my perceived sense of injustice secrete between us,
Only to find my grievance upstaged by the honey sucker,
Who, caring nothing for my solemnity, duly leaves me the sting of its tail.

A raucous laugh explodes from the crusty old man,
Now, there's a particular that's universally felt.

STRANGE JOY

You were buried alive, suffocated under a panacea
Of pain meds,
Did you see the last bit of light, disappearing?
There is no field of poppies to help in your transition,
No lake shore dreams to send you off in wonder,
Instead, we must sterilize your mind,
And float your body in sacred river of chemicals.

I cannot forget, nor forgive,

The lucid moments of lightness,
Aware, painfully aware of all that you were suffering,
Yet, unwilling to die,
Struggling against thoughts that once consumed
You.
Desperate lonely thoughts,
While we watched the life being drained from you,
Gently, drawing you further into that
Damp embrace,

Hush rage, let death suffuse you in
Strange kindness,
Pillow your pain, absorb all that you are,
Cry softly, while you fold your face into
The numbness.

Suffering must make its last stand,
And, you, whose force knew no bounds
Must acquiesce,
Surrender to death's strange mercies,

Shorter glimpses, now as you fade,

I want to save you!
Fight against the white darkness
That consumes my courage,
No more screams, only your deeps sighs,
You lie,
Suspended between breath and clay,
while we watch our choice reach its dark gestation,
Mother, I am no longer thy keeper.

Gone, emptied of struggle,
Your light fully extinguished,
Shrouded by stillness,
I am suffused by a strange peace,
Lingering,
Will your light reignite in a strange land?
Separated from the warmth of touch,
Hidden from the eyes that seek you,
Free of pain, anguish, will you
Awake? Awake with a lusty cry
And suckle on that strange joy
Fed on the nipple of eternity.

MIRIAM'S KADDISH

Nothing keeps us safe from the drag and pull
Of death's long shadow.
It's futile to attempt to nullify the effects with reason,
(Though it doesn't stop us trying).
Increasingly our world darkens with losses,
As we find ourselves moving closer to its shade.

The light of Miriam's soul dimmed out of sight,
But her song of jubilance and liberation echoes still,
Sister of flesh and heart, she had moved him, but not always,
Her spirit singing freely, joyously defiant,
Will continue to ghost him with the force of eternity,
Mr. Moses has retreated into the loneliness of grief.

Not stirring from his heart's cave, listening attentively
To the unremitting accusations of guilt and remorse.
His hope eclipsing, clouded over, sadly by regret,
The aged body poised in an unearthly contemplation,
Waiting silently, longing for a simple sign of redemption,
A soft word to ease the familiar wounds of sorrow.

His spirit bruised, bloodied against the wall of separation,
Presses in hard pressed against the darkness, waiting
At the chamber of his being for an echo of that song,
Head bowed, nursing gently the infancy of his sorrow,
Shouldering the loss, watching as the shade moves closer.

A LEAF FROM THE BOOK

The void spoke: and God, decidedly uncomfortable, listened,
Chaos muscled in with its constant frustration of being,
Random, unpredictable, refusing to be mollified or stilled,
Like the itinerant loneliness that pours in to happy thoughts.
Seeking to keep the knowledge that is born out of imperfection,

Dividing day from night, God bordered the walls of time,
Separating land from sea, space became discernably finite,
Parting Earth from heaven fixed the black and white of it all,
And, for a time, God's strategy appeared to work perfectly,
Order reigned and the sound of chaos and void were subdued.

Eve, tired reading of the endless secrets to a good partnership,
Wrestled with the pretense of being the apple of another's eye.
She could not settle the constant restlessness worming inside,
Adam's perfect adoration threaten to brick up her wandering curiosity,
She longed to taste the wonder of curious wild abandonment.

Adam drove to work in the usual fashion, careful, mindful
Of civic responsibility, kept his speed inside the legal limit.
In life, he deferred to the laws of physics, meta, and physical.
Satisfied to have achieved the goal for all, self-actualization,
In the pools of Eve's eyes, he saw himself happily complete.

God, pleased with the overall design of his creations, reposed,
Time and space, and a host of other delineations ticked over,
Spinning through each daily ritual with deftness and precision,
With stability and tranquility established through exactness.
However, there was a wrinkle in the folds of time and space.

Eve, disenchanted by the 12-step hype to a good relationship,
Admitted chaos, opened the borders to her soul to its vastness,
And, as she began undoing the illusion of order, skies greyed.
No longer narrowed down to a fixed point, her mind journeyed
Outwards, upwards, testing the margins of existing possibilities.

Undone by loneliness, Adam felt his need of Eve intensifying,
Re-made by uncertainty, she was now a myriad of complexities,
Coring out the familiar, she had in effect presented him with a gift,
Stripped of the known, he pilgrimaged towards her unknown,
They stumbled towards each other, unsure of their acute awareness.

Things have never returned, all is changed, wondrously changed,
Evolving incomprehensibly, glorious in ambiguity,
God watches as a new epoch wriggles in its mother's arms,
Wonderful in its inconsistencies, and God saw that it was good.

I PRAY THEREFORE I AM

So, what do you think of artificial life?
Bushy eyebrows have a language and a life of their own,
They can be so expressive but also confusing,
Are you harping back on this imposter syndrome again?
Life is never artificial if you're consciously living it.
Sometimes in our conversations words are like a riddle

I mean, A.I. Do you think we're playing God?
Knitted eyebrows can mean anything, good or bad,
Are you able to create a soul?
You can create an entity capable of making good decisions,
It may be even better at making the right choices,
Given how we are that could be a hell of a lot better.

Eyebrows unknot as lines of amazement crease upwards,
Mr. Moses' cheeky smile emerges from its inner sanctum,
So, in giving up the struggle to become better human beings,
We are creating a being, born out of logic and reason,
To engage with the moral and ethical complexities that burden us.
How fascinating.

When a child makes a mistake, they feel shame, guilt,
For the first time, they become aware of how imperfect life is,
A quickened soul moves them beyond innocence to experience.
Will A.I feel shame? Will it learn that to err is part of learning?
Can we shift the struggle to be good to another lifeform?
To be reasonably condemned to annihilation by our creation.

EPHEMERALITY

Tremulous billowy clouds fade to a whisper,
Hoarse in aspiration,
Tapering, they dissolve into blue nothingness
Their impermanency, unacknowledged,
Pass silently, without impression,
Some return with force and blustering,
Some re-appear angelic flight, playfully morphing
Into magical creatures of the imagination,
Enchantments of transformation, disappearing,
And their transformation another tease at the illusion of being.

THE DRUNKEN DUCK

I asked Moses what he thought of Noah and the flood,
A tale of survival during universal calamity seemed pertinent
To an age plagued by an invisible virus with many drowning
In their own secretions, and flowing in its terrible wake,
The usual damning sermons of divine judgment,

Surprisingly, given the gravity of the question, he laughed.
The joke, obviously at my expensive, left me peeved,

Sorry, no offense, when I think of that story it tickles me,
After the great deliverance of man and beast the old boy
Gets sozzled, and scares the living bejesus out of the family,
Can you imagine if that story happened these days?
Noah, once he saves the future of the human race,
Has one too many, and recklessly kills a couple of ducks,
Forever depriving us of that famous dish duck a l'orange.

The righteous man is never satisfied with being good,
Look at Jonah, he's proven right, and still a miserable sod,
It's no wonder the whale got indigestion and spat him out,
And, you gotta love Jeremiah's steampunk approach,
That prophet had a peculiar predilection for memes.
Or Esther, after she's pimped by her uncle, people are saved.
Makes you think twice about situational ethics,

*Stories like this remind us that even in our worst moments
God use science, religion, or whatever helps us endure,
Evil lies in our hands, we can destroy ourselves in a second,
But when we find ourselves on that precipice a voice of reason
Cries in the wilderness to prepare the way for commonsense.*

WHERE ANGELS FEAR TO TREAD

When God sang the universe into being,
With a curious tune that took on a life of its own,
There was rejoicing.
Many of those creative configurations harmonized,
Wonderfully romantic, empathic towards divinity,
Each one tugged at the heartstrings,

Some more independent notes could not,
Or would not, be constrained,
Syncopating their irregular, vigorous beauty,
They fearlessly burst into life, vibrantly,

Other notes, striving to compliment,
Ritually, ordered, and progressive in revelation,
Continued beyond the established tradition,
In a powerful surge of timbres, rising,
Pulsing, in vibrant, glorious tones,
The sound coursing through one another,
Creatively, searching out the creator's heart.

Letting those diverse sounds evolve was risky,
But God, forever the optimist, believed,
Even when some of the notes were a surprise,
Taking the long view, God, embraced his own
Darkness,
Choosing to feel the pangs of parenthood,

When suddenly, the music changed,
And, notes began to disappear into the abyss,
Their chords, dull and uneven, clunking together,
Discordant, and out of sync, God refused to
Stop listening,
The creation song was dying, and God grieved its loss,
Heaven fell silent,

A mournful lament ensued,
As the center of the sickness spread, outwardly,
The infection spread outwards, inwards,
Music changed, discordantly sorrowful,
Beauty revealed its ugly side to creation,
Goodness, and kindness mutated,
God watched as creation
Changing its tune.

THIS TRUTH WILL NOT SET YOU ON EDGE

Give me liberty, or give me death!

Mausoleums of concrete and steel
Frozen in time,
No longer softened by human voices.
Smiles . . . .
Washed away by the acrid air of disinfectant,
Tears alone remain, drying in the baking sun.

Anxiously, clinging to what was before,
Fearing what might come,
We wilderness people, with no oases in sight.
Hope for a prophet, a visionary,
Waiting, waiting . . . . for a sign.

Leaders, rarely lost for words, are mute,
Some, enamoured by their own star,
Sacrifice innocence for vainglorious acts.
In a game, where rules are not known,
They gamble numbers.
Others, unsure of their standing,
Break, when they should bend,
And bend while world breaks around them,

Empty streets, bars, churches, abandoned,
Mocking our love of comradery.
Billions of souls' wilt against the intruder.

All good people, crippled by quietness,
Hushed by a microscopic tyrant
(A bully of a thing).
Priests, Rabbis, Imams search their scrolls,
But none of them speak prophetically,
Alone, we stand before an infinitesimal giant
With no David in-sight.

Only the soothsayers with miracle cures,
Beguile us now with sweet street fantasies.
Filling the empty silences,
They pour their sickly babble into our ears,
To make us absorb their bleached-out truth.

FREEDOM

Freedom, he chewed on the word,
Salivating on its goodness,
As though wondering about its nutritional value.

Moses, a good foil to my impatience,
Refuses to be cajoled into sweetness or light,
But ruminators, like him, can be intensely frustrating.
They are so picky, when savouring each morsel,
The timer in my head would not stop beeping.

Personal or everyone's freedom?

Hmmm . . . . What was I thinking?
Personal, equates self-seeking, indulgent, selfish,
Head and eyes down, contrite,
I spat out the altruistic seed at his feet.

He summed me up in a wistful look.

What's good for me, is good enough for everyone,
Don't you think?
We all hunger for the same things
And sometimes the only way we can get them
Is by sharing what we have with those who have not.

Having masticated and digested my humble pie,
He belched his satisfaction in a smile.

A SYMPATHETIC FUSION

Joseph didn't have a charmed childhood
His family's values weren't all that good,
Dad, the ardent schemer, was a true believer,
But he played the odds like a cunning deceiver,
Joseph, whose notions were above his station,
Riled his brothers into an active demonstration,
They mobbed and trafficked the coatless Joe
Alienating him to a land where he would grow.

When realized, dreams are costly but saving things,
They charm and entice you with the gifts they bring,
Inflating your pride, they connive to set you apart
If you endure them, they will surely break your heart,
Hapless Joe soon found deliverance in his dreams
Only after enduring the cost of their tragic schemes.

A man of power, eminent in stature he became,
No longer recognizable, he would never be the same,
Transcending his past, he became a gifted outsider,
Trading new ideas with the knowledge of an insider,
Joseph's scheming became a part of the dreaming,
It was this need for a tribe helped put anger aside,
And, bring the healing to those who held ill-feeling.

PASSING SHADOWS

So much of him has been lost to the years,
Though the face still bears traces of handsomeness,
Occasionally, I glimpse signs of his youthful prowess,
The patriarchal body, now heavy with godawful time,
Circumvents the usual barbs of sedentary life
When one gazes on the patina of one stained with mystery.

Why does this fragile beauty sadden me?
Joy, riddled with casual fear, is evanescent, light of foot,
Its existence, something that is increasingly dimming,
Until it finally disappears into the fog of passing seasons.

What is this thing I call my soul?
That piece of me that refuses to keep up or fall back
On command,
That bit of me that affords me no truce in its arsenal of jibes,
Skewering my romantic attachment to an elusive authentic self.

Moses is more distracted than ever,
Is he afraid?
Has some unseen enemy made him pensive?
Forcing his soul to move from the trenches to the front line,
Where he has begun to ascend over the top, where all life lies.
The scant threads to his existence have begun to wear thin,
Disquieted by the harsh reality of loss outweighing any gains.

Nothing remains as a constant, everything trickles down
Against the granite face of God etched into our souls,
Weeping on the feet of all that is washed away into yesterday.

Abstracted, the craggy face peers into the nothingness,
Where cloistered thoughts cannot flee the barren privacy
Of doubt,
Maybe his authentic self is retreating from my scrutiny,
Do I make him self-conscious as he does me?
The sad, beautiful Moses trickles down through my soul
As the one constant selfless warrior clambering
Over the top and into no man's land.

HIDE AND SEEK

God danced the seven veils of creation
Revealing all and nothing.

Love in abstraction reveals all of me,
Love in particular finds me rushing for fig leaves.

NOT A WORD

I wanted to write a song about the rushes
But its style was out of tune
And, the wind blew through it.
I wanted to sing of the wild mountain thyme
But was told not to cry in my beer
Because the cynics would see through it.
I tried to sing of love and how it never knew me
You called it nostalgic and blue
As though I'd already knew it.

Your song's been sung so many times before
No matter how much you try to construe it.

I tried to write a poem about love's endurance,
Words, unglued, became estranged,
Good words, familiar friendly ones
Became foreigners,
Jarring each other in grandiose jibes.
Their mealy-mouthed disdain
Edges me towards the incomprehensible,
Or drags me back to safety
Punctuating my thoughts without stopping.

Alone, my search gamboling,
Stretching every inaudible syllable
So, the world can see it,
Its jangling tune, abrasive and bold,

Out of sync in disharmonious verses
So, that all can hear it,
My cleft spirit, disfigured in speech,
Assails the ear with a monstrous lexicon
So, garbled that one can feel it,
Must I swallow back those guttural sighs
And bury my trite humanity
Until someone comes to heal it.

BLANK STARE

I looked into the eyes, there were no words
The lips of the eyelids struck dumb.
I thought I knew every little inflexion of those smiling eyes
But I was wrong.
The accented gaze muted, replaced by a stony stare
With enough rock in them to punish any onlooker.

I tried to write a poem today
But the words stank to the high heavens,
They rotted as quickly as I put them down,
Covered with a strange blight, festering pus
As though the evil genie within us all
Waited to be released and wreak havoc
In a tidy garden of words.

Language can be so pungent,
When you have a lover's quarrel with the Word?

Remember the joke, the jibe, the hot knife
Running through the butter,
It didn't hurt then.
Oozing out in delight, dripping with saucy subtext,
With the occasional nick, playing a little too close
To the bone.

There it is again that blank stare,
Turning the onlooker's heart to stone,
Enough said.

RAPTURED IN YELLOW

When I was a young man a butterfly flew at me with all its yellowness,
And, somewhere inside my head seeds began to take root.
Soon, a silly yellow intoxication infiltrated my heart,
Fluttering ideas tickling my thoughts, making me
                                  laugh at the universe,

I was giddy, for a time, when that yellow pollinator flew my way,
Fluttering nervously, as he did, trembling with excited gaiety,
Approaching, retreating, hungry for something, yet resisting,
Landing briefly on me, lightly touching, intoxicating
                                  my whole universe.

For a time, I believed you felt that kick within me,
Lustfully dancing, engorging your being in my nectar,
Still, there was a part of you flitting erratically, unwilling to rest,
Lightly touching upon those shared moments of union,
But never allowing stillness to woo you into submission,
Fearing my desire tarnish your brilliance,
                                  And you fall from the sky.

When we separated a fountain of yellow burst out of me.
Something in me was in you, and somewhere in you was me,
                        I was sad.
The life of the universe, its yellowness cursed us with devotion,
Badgering us to seek out a hallowed place to worship.
Now, you idly drift between others, no longer gaily fluttering
Watching me watch your pale, tepid neutral resignation,
                                  Lost in universal monochrome.

THE NIGHTINGALE'S SONG

The little nightingale sang a song of freedom.
Its voice was clear and the joyous sound echoed unceasingly.
And soon the world over was captured by its beauty,
People who had never heard the nightingale sing before
Stopped to listened to the enchanting melody.
Good people, cheered by the song,
Happily, welcomed the sacred sound into their hearts.

A bear passing heard it's song in a casual breeze
Though he could not decipher the meaning of the song,
It was the strength of the singer that irked him most.
Roaring brusquely, brandishing his immense bulk, he cursed air.

Sending all the other animals and birds into hiding.

Incensed by the bird's defiance and lack of respect,
The bear determined to put an end to the nightingale's singing,
besieged the beautifully feathered bird in its nest,
Muscled its brute form onwards to the tower of song,
Bearishly tearing at everything and everyone that got in its way.
Until it finally lay siege at the beautiful feathered one's nest.

All around eyes watched as the bear came dangerously close,
To obliterating the bird's home place.
They watched as innocent blood fell from the massive paws.

Refusing to be silent, the nightingale continue to sing,

It's warbling heart could not, would not surrender to the beast.
A soulful pathos warmed in the hearts of all who heard it.
Infuriated, the bear threatened to kill little bird and any other bird who sang like it if it didn't stop with its song,
And, for a moment, the bird stopped singing,
And, for a moment the world was silent, Angels wept.
And, for a moment, all that could be heard was the bearish growl of antipathy.

Thinking himself victorious, the bear's snarl boomed out.
Making the very earth shudder beneath the brute's bloody trail.

Strained by its resistance, the little bird tried to sing once more.
But its song was bereft of joy, its hope bruised.
Laughing to himself, the bear rejoiced at the perceived sound of defeat.
Until a ghostly sound began to rise about him,
Wave after wave of voices, rising in unison, from every direction,
Drowned out the raucous growls of the bear,
And, soon the air was full of passionate singing,
Across the planet, angels and people began to sing in harmony
To the song of the nightingale.

STRANGE FIRE

A strange fire ignited in me,
It's rage, unchecked, untamed,
Burning every good thought to ashes,
I watched as Roman columns fell to the ground,
Nothing good escapes such flames.

Arriving at Mr. Moses' house, I was smouldering.
His eyes scrutinized me for any sign of life,
But all that was me had died in the fire,
Only a ghostly residue of what was remained,
A restless spirit with unfinished business.

You found us then. No fun getting up here.
Lots of switchbacks up the mountain can take it out of you.

Aaron, his mangy cat, wouldn't shut up meowing,
Crawling under my legs, the feline showed no respect for the dead.

The missus made us some lovely cheese bread.
By the looks of you, you could use a bit of sustenance.

Aaron's constant preaching finally got my attention,
His soul purred with a satisfied hymn of approval.

A door opened, followed by a waft of delicious smells.
Silhouetted in the in light, Mrs. Moses beckoned us to follow,
Channelled by that generous smile, I quietly obeyed.

A lavish feast warmly greeted our senses,
Amid the embers, and as the smoke thinned,
I sensed that something of the temple was still intact, untouched.
Mr. Moses blessed and broke the bread
And, in that holy place, I felt satisfied in the Amen.

TEMPLE

When a bullet grazed my thoughts
The sky emptied itself, and, for a moment,
I saw myself as called, chosen.
A survivor of the brute force of being alive.
Touching the right temple, I'm animated,
Touching the left temple finds me quizzical,
Between these temples lies the remnants
Of a forgotten paradise,
Ditches of overgrown ideas, adrenalin junkies
Ripe with PTSD, digging themselves into an
Early grave.

A star exploded in my brain, a supernova
Of gigantic proportions,
Shooting through my right-sided left brain
Shiny tiny pieces of debris in-between the temples,
Twinkling fragments of a star in epilogue,
Glittering now as little orbs pulsating, puzzling,
Perplexing in nature, blinking as if In Memoriam,
Worshipped by the right, they have become
Angels of light on the left.

www.ingramcontent.com/pod-product-compliance
Lightning Source LLC
Chambersburg PA
CBHW061509040426
42450CB00008B/1533